Tethered to the Earth

TYLER FARRELL

salmonpoetry

Published in 2008 by
Salmon Poetry,
Cliffs of Moher, County Clare, Ireland
Website: www.salmonpoetry.com
Email: info@salmonpoetry.com

Copyright © Tyler Farrell 2008

ISBN 978-1-903392-81-2

All rights reserved. No part of this publication may be reproduced or transmitted in any form or by any means, electronic or mechanical, including photography, recording, or any information storage or retrieval system, without permission in writing from the publisher. The book is sold subject to the condition that it shall not, by way of trade or otherwise, be lent, resold or otherwise circulated without the publisher's prior consent in any form of binding or cover other than that in which it is published and without a similar condition, including this condition, being imposed on the subsequent purchaser.

Cover artwork: Douglas Koepsel
Cover design & typesetting: Siobhán Hutson

For Joan

Acknowledgments

Thanks are due to the editors of the following in which some of these poems have previously appeared:

The Blue Canary, Natural Bridge, The Recorder, Salt Fork Review, Front Range Review, Yemasse, The Jabberwock Review, and *The Book of Irish American Poetry* (University of Notre Dame Press).

I only felt that here once more was the treachery of Nature and that in the country nothing is what it seems and everything is something else.
—Austin Clarke

Have not all races had their first unity from a mythology, that marries them to rock and hill?
—W. B. Yeats

Contents

I. Northern Wisconsin

On Seeing a Girl Pluck a Four Leaf Clover	13
Many Hours After the Night Began, I Walked Home In The Dark	14
A Walk In A Field Ten Miles Outside of Town	15
On Hearing That While Ice Fishing Alone, A Boy Drowned in Long Lake	16
Ode to a Stranded Horse	17
Transporting a Cow to the Mainland	18
For A Winter Scarf That Has Stayed With Me Despite My Forgetfulness in Recognizing Its Strength and Devotion	20
When We Were Children of the Woods	21
From Downy Hill	23
An Auction at Harbor Lights	24
The Altar of Forests, The Palace of Fallen Trees	26
Letter From An Old Tree	28
On Seeing a Man Painting the Lake	30
The Sun, I Could	31
To a Pair of Shoes Left in My Office	33
Thoughts on Leaving South Shore	35
Two White Hands	36
Broken Thorn Trees at an Unmarked Grave	37
On Reading An Article About The Death of The Written Word	38
From an Aerial View, A Map of the Northwoods	40
The Sky a Living Grey	41
Reflecting on a Poem Written By A Girl from Willow Point	42

The Lake Is A Pistol in Winter	44
For the Ghost of the Northwoods	46
An Hour of Broken Light	47
Voices from Cold County	48
Letter from Madeline Island	49

II. *Europe Like a Forest Praying*

Arriving at Atocha Station	53
A Sudden Sense of Panic From Watching a Wasp Wither and Die	54
Three Women Who Wept	55
Elegy for Father Louie	56
To Frank O'Hara in Heaven	58
For an Old Woman Who Lives in Salema	59
On Seeing the Ghost of Frank O'Hara at the Louvre	60
A Garden in Morning: Poem on James Joyce's Birthday	62
On Being Lead Into St. James Church, Shere	63
Poem Written On A Cigarette Box	64
This Darkened London	65
Paseo de Orson Welles	66
You Will Know It When Comes, You Will Forget It When It's Over	67
Guernica in Flames at the Picasso Museum, Barcelona	68
Galway and the Smokeless Pubs of the New Millennium	69
Into Europe by Rail—First the Daylight Pulled at Length	70

I.
Northern Wisconsin

On Seeing A Girl Pluck a Four Leaf Clover

Past the sun,
a lighted damp field of trefoil
was seasoned,
lasted, color in abundance.
Glass harnessed
bell atop a field of brick red
energy sheds
breaking in early afternoon.
In the acetelyne glow
of midday's protuberant eyes,
she christened our small
outside crowd.

Many Hours After the Night Began, I Walked Home In The Dark

I heard willows blown down lake shore drive,
footsteps following me from third street.
I noticed sounds at the community center corner.
A faint hum of trains leaving town, slump and heavy
thug momentums wait for an empty bank. They move
in and out of sense, loud then soft. The moon gleams
on the roof of the Presbyterian church, handled chime
1:00 a.m. I saw a few kids on that corner yesterday.
A fire hydrant opened this afternoon on Main street.
Now the moonlight leaves chicory flower pavement
colors. A car closes in until past and I pull my hat
to cover my ears. The lethal air falls over the marina,
spreads through downtown like fog in the morning,
hovering until noon when seagulls move shores, leaf
pebbles away from shops, windows, red brick town
hall towers and navy blue soldiers on the mural wall.
The tires in a field like unkempt graves, a small white
candle in the window, a feather bed and canopy under
servant stars, times of small towns in past lives. A black
wingtip on the ground, the sole's wearing thin. I saw it
last week while looking for old books at the library,
watching thick men sit in chairs and read papers, chew,
yawn and play mean corduroy on crossed legs. Windows
are covered with brown paper burlap. The boy at the
Co-op is fondling the vegetables while an old lady sits
in a basement room staring into a flickering corner.
There might as well be bars on her windows instead
of glowing lights, angel hair, TV trays and E-Z chairs.
The light from a red neon sign sits in a puddle near
the cracks in the funeral home parking lot. The house
down the road is still for sale. The heat from a chimney
draws up into the clouds, forms words in air, gives
light to the moon and sends frail frost to grey flowers.

A Walk In A Field Ten Miles Outside of Town

Wells in coldest winters
run like large thickets
of crimson roses on tall
pergolas. Song book
birds, slump trail feet
play like lutes in spring
villas, marble fountains,
the wind like an opiate.
The yellows draw gallant
canaries, daggers swing
as acts of darkness, winding
in between the bends of the
Bad River. Stolen light grazes
in fields of fairies, track rocks
and rakes with blond heather
torn from blue earth, planted
under tire piles, logs leaned
against a faded barn door.
The bent space of a man's
overcoat on a tree branch
wobbles like the angry lake,
a wintry eye tapered grey.
There are proud breaths
over the next hill, sun silt
mixed with clouds aslant.

On Hearing That While Ice Fishing Alone, A Boy Drowned in Long Lake

It seemed unlikely, unmentioned.
A crowd gathered around, moving
like fleas bites, wrapped in pea
colored blankets. The remote light
from the top of the hill where
the Trappist Monastery was built.
When the dead awaken they will
burn blue like the heron, blend into
bewildered skies, a muttered glance
still sound from the wind chime
hung from tall winterized trees like
a bell rung from a chipped white
steeple. A fog crept from the north,
postponed the search until morning
when hidden suns burn water
droplets from the air. He was half
submerged like icicles and old
pillars from a small dock stuck into
frost bitten mud, belief in birds
for food, draped loosely over a bed.
Where isobars dipped into fertile
sleet storms, rumbling branches left
apart from a limp body, the smell
of wet leaves struggling to burn
while we bear our fathers on our
backs. The fish from first flights
freeze into ice while eyes look
to the light sky to wonder where
their life has gone. A thick earth
to hide in. A burial whispered
beneath this clear, broken stone.

Ode to a Stranded Horse

Madeline Island tears in the wind
with scattered tarps
over Tom's Burned Down Cafe.
We plant trefoil in days
says less than we want hold our
arms high in the air to dry
them. How much to bring a horse
on the ferry? He is standing
over there in the weeds
munching on flowers as necessary
as a newel in a circular staircase.
I wonder how he got here,
traded by trappers long ago
or wild like a pinto, his eyes
the color of corn meal.
Maybe he was mailed c.o.d.
The post office is on the banks
of the south shore beach.
The mailman sorts letters by hand.
Winter rains have finally ended,
the day runs bright skies smiling
overhead. The horse suddenly
looks up at me chewing
his clover, probably wondering
why I almost stare through
his body. I think about riding
him all over the island, our own
search party on days when
no one could be found,
silver shadows of settlers
bonfires making pines
into a red and orange ceiling
for the earth and its little lights,

windows of old photographs.
Instead I watch him bound back
into the trees, his shape
disappearing in the leaves.
Back to his home on this island.
Never able to swim for it
even if he wanted to.

Transporting a Cow to the Mainland

A third day of island mooring rumpled,
watered by rains as thick as the sea.
Every soul in ripple soaked and limped
lighthouses with a cracked window
warning. No cheer and shifter of home.
The cunning weather had kept us
in sensible rabble, a crest above the strand.
The men stood with donkeys ready to trade.
A goat or two, a basket of fish, a sack
of wool, pigs and chickens, the boats
on the key, a sailor to Dingle Bay.
My three Uncles, myself, my sister's
husband were at halt on a cliff top.
A price for a drink, a trade, the slaughter
for another minute like a battle ended
with a bit of rascal luck, a scarecrow
instead of a man. I saw a butcher kick
a sheep stone dead. He then took a knife
from his pocket and let out her blood,
wrung her heart. We left the cow in the
morning and breakfast with the traders
was a shop like gulping itself down
so we could leap back to the island
with more whiskey, a shilling more
than a pound. The crew had melted like
the foam on a river, the shame of the rest.
I sent a blessing for sixpenny worth.
A week from today would be the same.
The whole blessed world was then.

For A Winter Scarf That Has Stayed With Me Despite My Forgetfulness in Recognizing Its Strength and Devotion

Soon I rise and see a simple day turning into sunlight
and rain that softly lands on my windshield. It leaves
imprints like glare bubbled blues and yellows
that I have tragically not seen since the end of summer.
Joan's scarf cradles my neck well into the new spring. I hide
inside my car for a small morning to think of when home
will be more permanent. There is an enormity of life
when risks are taken and each season passes to let
us know of small time like still days that seem lost
in last year's fallen leaves and cabin fevers. Soon
there will be lawn parties, bitter joy, a hitched
past while a friend reads a libretto aloud and guests
sigh and think of moving to a bar or going home
early in the evening to look alive and talk of work
and books, the sorted plans for the last free summer.
There is a mounting panic over boredom and dreadful
overindulgence about the ways of happiness filled
with the goings on of past friends who are now rivals.
The car begins to freeze in its spot and the scarf
has been like a security blanket in a time of uncertainty.
Vaguely I hear the torn wind with colored sounds
in a purifying wave of exposed light, stumbling breaths,
stars captured like a darkness emptied onto a white
background. I feel a renewal around my neck.
I feel the morning with a quick-witted impunity.

When We Were Children of the Woods

In my first childhood,
the forests of Roundwood near the reservoir
of Westfield was where I played
with cousins and summer friends.
We heard the dizzying whirl
from a western wind like
the blowing of a blacksmith's bellows,
the fires and fumes of a night time
sky in a return journey through darkness.
The blue clay mysteries, the flooded
gleam of the moon, a small grotto that we
admired with our heart's tongue. We breathed
in with spirit lungs, heard the roar of flame,
the rustle of last year's leaves. The oblong
trees felled in winter slanted and brittled
by bugs, robins nests and woodpecker holes.
We told fire myths and danced
like nymphs in the lined shadows
of the obscure forest shouting furtive
and demure glances to the owls
looking down upon our little
plays acted out in the pine needle clearing
complete with logs to sit on and a bucket
for donations, but often rusted over
by water drops and dewy sheaths
wrapped in early morning. The slanted lawn
was used to rest and bat pine cones
into the tops of little evergreens,
a safety line for erosion. A deep hollow
was covered in brown moss like the bushy beard
of our Grandma's neighbor, so we named it
Gus and sat at its opening
like a clubhouse gang, a secret handshake

hedgerow, brighter than the dreary ones back home.
The natural footpath was lined with hawthorn
and guarded with thorns. I thought another
leafy plant looked pretty, but after picking
it was told by my Uncle that it was
called Dead Man's Hand and I never
plucked it again. The grand and flooded
tree like outdoors of slopes and broken
pricker leaves that embedded in palms
like a light rain refreshing a dry pocketed land.
The weary road home brought
simple shacks and terraced houses onto the edge
of natural and formative red and brown
greens, the foliage that once ruled the earth.
The road would break in dusty light
between farmland and city hums of tires
on gravel roads and then traded for crumbling pavement.
There was a simple protection
to wooded alcoves, tall beckoning trees,
branches that consumed and obscured our sight.
They would eventually disappear and every year
I waited and watched for a time when I could
go back as an adult and inhale
the children's forest air and splintered sun
to anesthetize the way they did on those
patient and fairy-tale summer nights.

From Downy Hill

The night is a procession of summers. Eyes with a perfect
soul often lift in spring. Downy hill like a glass
sanctuary unstuck to flowers from a temple field. Light
in between thickets and trees.

Always a black shape. Navy balloons on the edge of sky,
while dances cling to the four corner girls
in plain dresses. Overspilled solstice and the wind
woven from an old curtain.

A shy flower opens at a stone path cornered by rings
melted in golden rays. Braided hair in the hills, now
flesh cries out and winds away. The day's head
lies down to sleep.

Thumbs of boys belong to horse hair grass, a mother's face
studies the smudge in the sky. Clouds without wings,
the secret voice and medicinal thorns on the bride's side
of the river. Her groom waits.

An Auction at Harbor Lights

Waves of music from my pockets roar like
light homes on dark tides. Three sentences held
together with sun for horses freed from fields
to pull weary dancers in melting snow.
These bloodied feet sink into glens, march
out from white tongues in the sky. North star
mission to crawl out of caves, sail like bended
knees and prayers for the end of sleep, evil
fires that dream of cold hearts moaning bones.
Blind and wonderful advertisements in clouds
of the coming stone eyes of the lake, water
running again into marshes and sticking to
barrels collected for the junk man out at the
end of Highcourt road.

Blue waters under the snow escape like steam
from our mouths. Boats crowd into the stale
of wooden bridges, pale days of early dusk and
a fog as humid as one in late summer. The light-
house man examines iron rails, drinks like a
Wicklow man before the rain blows him away.
A farmhouse in moonlight with fields grown
hot from small showers. There is someone at
the fair, wild grass, and crowds like a simple
trail of footsteps in the snow soon to be traded
for a commotion of wild sunlight. A small
dealer yells at daybreak, holding numbers
like flames. Young and old birds squawk and
trade, blind light as loud as a bellows hooked
to an old trumpet.

Lucky like a horseshoe in piles as large as coal,
stag wood, brown rags and bad shoes. The harbor
looks like an island laid out in the sun to dry
before the tide drops this workshop into the marsh.
A forest of postcards sent from Spain when laughs
rested in the fade of the dew. This strange beauty,
a lit candle like a shadow that tumbles into a
heart and a drum. This blessed sleepless land,
heavy flowers and countless middlemen
in constant search for the sea.

The Altar of Forests,
The Palace of Fallen Trees

The planter watched rabid
trees fallen blossoming into roads
where wind had danced
with sheets of rain, hail in thunders,
the black stretch of bays.
Hikers ask of daylight, rotten
silly lines of deer treading
upon the sinister light, dirt covered
grass hills, berms folded
in rain. The world is a basement,
difficult to collect itself
in such hardened air, restless dew,
larks and crane dipping
into lakes, ring pools and mortuary
grounds left of spark.
The image is a primitive dream,
layers of clay, startled
treetops, fastened like a harness
to its source. They bend
at the horizon, dredge up water
and slip themselves back
into the sky, the clouds at lines
drawn by the ridge
of fishermen closed off from an island.
There is a wind sigh,
a ghost in the eyes of the sun,
lit and heathered
by secret hands that reach for
the edge of cliffs fallen
away in spirit, epic graves covered
in rocks, moss, damp

willows with leaves thinner than
spindles, a black lizard
opens like a violet, trundles its legs
borrowed to the well.
I will trade you for water, trample
the dirt at your grave,
cover the sun like Jupiter, softly
jumble the woods.
The glittered boughs laugh at us,
springs and snares
of blackbird pudding, the edge of
an orchard and windows
like tissue shaped moths, a sunlit
whimper from the cabin.
It is time to return. When screech owls
cry the themes of night.
The eyes were gone, the dried earth
lay barren, a fallen scope
trained my sight on the slanted elms.
It was an earth sermon,
divine light preached from the edge
of the world's pulpit.
The language bathed in bells, stories
of sinners, demons, a hung
soul stolen like retreat assailed in
night and day. These venial
sins torment the world below, confess
those fears. A natural state
of grace, a ponderous throng and berth.

Letter From An Old Tree

Dear children,
I climbed two rounds
in a green ravine
tired whispered tales
from sunlight
down the close side
of a little doom.

Dark like hermits
in moonlight stalls.

This flood was a
hurricane, swirling
bark like a hayloft
in a windstorm.
The cottage fires
light a short cut
to the lake.

      I used
to see you leap
the sea, the tides
now doomed
to break when
thunder slept
along the quay.
We peeled cork
from a trunk
sinking slowly
in a keyhole
made of damp
earth.

Cracks like we
drown in oceans.
Confess like
clouds and travel
no more above
my tallest arm.
Mark this spot
with play and
ragged spirit.

On Seeing a Man Painting the Lake

He looks over the fires of glimpsed sunlit
pines, his shadow lies bent on the water.
With tallied paint cans, brushes, thinner
from the bulkhead under his kitchen windows,
he pours greens and blues from the delicate
shore, vats of land, the winter cloth
soon drawn from the loom. The calm dawn
is around us. We are the only ones
to see these clearlake mysteries, tops of trees,
a shot fall breeze knocking into whitecaps,
the steady copper color edges, heather
vines, the smoke of prayerful souls
seeping from the factory into the air.
My eyes water cold drops, then soften
to drizzle. He holds his hand like a wand,
until the world is canvassed, smoke light
dim morning burnt bright on the sky rim.

The Sun, I Could

The sun is gold
like it was melted to ingot,
transported seaward,
erected on North Island,
left to melt under
warm weather billowed skies.
I could glean the shine
from the sun reapers.
I could well grow
like a statue erected
heavenward, illuminated
all hours. I could see
the curve of the world's
tonsure like a priest
in a candle lit room.
These graceful pillars,
pretty veils in frenzy,
visions of sweet lighted
scent, as bright as a
single lamp-post lurking
on darkened street.
I could name the stars,
small mill ponds,
streets with closed eyes.
I could let the world
beckon, drape it's virtue
with night, a ripple
and glance. Bright coils
wrap us with warmth,
robed like a lime white
queen. I could laugh
like a crow, let the sun
weather the stones.

I could set a girl
on the moon, a field
of nettles hurled
into light. I could shout.
I could trade myself
nameless, immoderate
tones, mouth gaped
in wonder. I could
succeed. I could humor
myself. I could throw
anguish out the door,
wait for it to return.
I could undo. I could
hear the church bells
like a Mahler symphony,
the soul black lining,
street news, cobbled
rumors and cardplayers.
An open air shrine
like that of St. Bridget.
I could leave behind
my small wooden crutch,
kindling. A luminary
glows in my head.
I could let it show.

To a Pair of Shoes Left in My Office

I thought you would have
run away when she left you
next to a bag of papers,
discarded laces and all.
The window has opened
the tongues, dried them
like hanging grapes,
tattered webs outside
my window under silver
house shingles, smudged
rose on the sills. The creek
has frozen early again,
rocks in ice as if dropped
through glass, cracked
and weaved, big eyed faces
float to the top of buckthorn
forests. A can of pencils
has tipped next to you,
in a corner, left from the
beginning of this wasted
year. The fingertaps on
thick wooden doors will
do no good, the wind runs
leaves like lashes. I see
you walk in the snow,
footprints in permanent
cement like writing your
name just before the grey
light reaches a threshold.
No going back, no erasure.
I feel you across the room.
You want to be thrown
away, at least set down

in another space, a new shape
outside of dark hallways.
Not even the clouds can
do a thing about your stare.

Thoughts on Leaving South Shore

Oval faces of birds resting in the ruins of midday haze,
tear poetry in their eyes. A forest worker missing
two fingers, brilliant morning in April.

Stern canvas shelter laths, listless air over quaysides
circling hours like temples of mystery. Calm endless
waters voyaged gentle in trances.

Dreamlike races, manner of habits, the face of Canada
disturbed by the sun. Pale train hawthorn hung
over gates, the sun shining a sallow greeting, full

leaf trees, summer plans and fresh lemon for your
throat. The rule of names christens the land clotted
with dark canals.

Under season windows lay the road and rows of trees,
shadows impassive, a slow ripple from a front door
and an unsure way to feel.

Two White Hands

I am watching two white hands full of early red roses.
Pride from the children comes in screams. We pretend
not to hear them as boats fill with water.

We saw the girls put out the trash. In blinking light
the speech is in the wind. Bells ring in steeples
signaling my departure. I risked miles of wilderness
to sit in a bar.

The memory of fall will hurt me most, the twilight
guns in the sky, the countenance of air among red roofs.
It passes in and out of flat land.

Lakes speak when rivers pour. Roads look like ribbons,
tower rooms at dead ends. Trees fall into traffic,
unbroken lines of log trucks like waiting hawks.

Silence like a monument, water posed under the sun
like deep sky. I sit in pools under a park bench,
the home moved from my face.

I see a window open in January. A moment shines
on cross streets, snow like white hands. Often lives
are saved by one person.

Broken Thorn Trees at an Unmarked Grave

Air moves like a drawbridge,
a compass passes us
this way. Thrown
wooden battens on fire
from a lighting strike,
dark rails sent by the plain eyes
of a rocky path. We soak
in restless reflections on the grass
muddied with snow.
Smoke burns the clouds
to rain, slow smells
carried with a hand
towards sunset. Sand from the wind
prints out rough edges
of wood, ashes of earth
carried underground.
The sun is a pale garrison
hidden like the large eye
of a wolf in a dark forest,
leaves frozen to the ground.
Stones carved as hinges
reeling the gates, consoling the grieved.
We can hear the hushed
cheers in the trees.
They tell us to stay.
They feed us with spirits.

On Reading An Article About The Death of The Written Word

The daily rejoice,
sun curled clusters
like a flame
in the shadow of night.
The dawn of flagstones
seen in dreams,
wholly in tune blended
with hushed music,
days, nature like
powerful faces drawn
into the middle
of the next line,
thorns from reform.
Those faces in repose,
method breaths,
other poets returned
to stack books,
sell siding, hermits
of public dominion.
Tonic for wordlessness,
ailments glitter
in the lungs freed with
simple idleness, tiny
golden delicate grace.
Night time reminds us
of briars, astir nature
flown wind aloft.
Grab onto its wings
for the sake of a page.
Last seat juniors
soon play seniors,

froglike, pale green
looks, river smells
hurt timeless lands.
The brave left weeping.
The rest existed
to swim in the wind.

From an Aerial View,
A Map of the Northwoods

This map drowns in white. North lakes
swallowed by Superior when large eyes cross
over bad lines of winters trembling under
shelter of grey birds called barbed
wire. There on the perch for a few months,
an agony in ice. The kissing neighbors
like dots in window wells where the green
house slants into the river while barrels fill
with artesian water. Frozen buckets like
clear luminaries, candles snuffed by
the slightest breeze whispering names
of the night. Frosted trees, snowmobiles at
the darkest hour and islands landing on
new tarmac when ripples carved the shore
many miles from the mainland. Students at
the Black Cat run off like rain water
when drips land in back alleys with no sun,
grease lines drowning into the rusted grates
of the sanitation department like a phony
slight horizon swung open to blind
the white of the ground and dirt beneath
these grim April clouds. No one can see past
the wooden prison of elms, but last night
we all cheered the boring glare of moonlight.

The Sky a Living Grey

Snowflakes

the ides of March
forgot

produce this broken
island

flagged in north
sea

Wisconsin. Paintings
projected

into the sky,
strokes

expanded like arrows
over

calm endless waters
dreamlike

a race of manner
habits

disturbed by the sun.
Shivering

like ornaments on a
tree,

the lights baptizing
our

winter sores now
a basket

of desires.

Reflecting on a Poem Written
By A Girl from Willow Point

She was the full shine of daylight.
Brownstones and bog flowers widened her eyes.
Enlivened tone with a voice of sweetened missions
in order to identify us. Spoken out loud
ruined in our faces, a lorded stare,
a minimal lower gate sipped from broken
thoughts like cups cracked in sandboxes.
She wrote and read me a poem called "Home"
with lines taken from her youth. I heard her say,
> The whole crowd flushed in
> sober china white,
> when nightingales turned blue.
> The leaves in burden stairs
> flip flurries in empty symptom sills.
> Defy the light and graze the hornets nest,
> scowls from yesteryear.
> The garrets and still divination
> glide in crisis like kites
> melting in air, a streamer diving
> to the ground, spun skittered horses
> with bent sun eyes,
> damp whispers and blistered grass
> like coatsleeves frayed in dark closets.

I ran into the above room loud as thunder.
My eyes reddened like sloe gin,
oranges on a burnished wooden table
hidden in the sunrays of fallen afternoons.
Brightness washed out sidelines, country grins
like those from a shop keeper in overalls, dust city
hats and museums carved for silent lichens.
Flown home flustered, the surgery of black diamonds,

windows leapt like rosebuds at night.
She looked vulpine in her turn of a fall coat,
the sands as course as silt, her eyes like a cat.
We left each other in the street where we spread
oozing blue smoke, petals, the tiny cogs
of a clock sputtering in quiet bolts
as I gargled her perfume in my throat.
Her stride north was faceless as I had
forgotten her light green eyes until just now.

The Lake Is A Pistol in Winter

Sixteen sail at blue noon
frozen winter waters.

Suns shine early
embers in gridiron.
Shadows like shawl holes
covered with weeds and snow.

We rouse the town
when the light is warm
and bleed ourselves
into cold covered streets.
Old silence be beaten
back to the sea.

Children yell
like winds bellow
on streets for narrow
lamps, red splattered
curtains,
worn windows.

Even the moss prays
it will return.

Some homes starve
this time. They buckle
in the snow.
Shovels
upside down
in drifts.

The smoke sounds
to the sky.
Sheds empty with
shotgun shell fever.

What miracles.

For the Ghost of the Northwoods

She invented herself
dancing in the streets
until night fell and
smelled of snow and ice,
when northern lights
illuminate the lake.

We went pale in dark
trembling woods,
bodiless and slow
silver burnt into a
black and white photo
taken in terror.

Our hands stained like
harvests from widened
doors and firesides.
Wet darkness unable
to speak, only a drift
in wind forms rain.

She spoke like a dark
glove pulled over
a white hand, shuddered
as angels do when
masks cover the new
rituals from oval skies.

Chains in shadow
hooded by stars she
disappeared like a grip
of ice in Spring and
perfect silence led us
in hand over hills.

An Hour of Broken Light

This county rustles with lightness a pulse,
lawless backyards and vines hung like
summer rainwater on old concrete walls.
Suns trickle and bury tall flame spots,
black ash in urns made of crossroads,
emptiness, dark thickets and willows.
Like a dream in the desert chiseled from
sandrock and seekers loaded by tides
waking alone and stunted by the shore.
Clouds roll doubt through highwinds,
hazards of youth and regrets of age
this soft blame a confession, a waving
hand sighing like the breeze of streams
captured in our hands. Some moments
last longer in a city's relief. Step lightly
through these natural minefields of life.

Voices from Cold County

We are pulling thorns from our door, dream lights of swallows and loons that burn symbols like sunlight on a winter glaze of ancient land, fields that dot the powder blue sky curved on Sundays. The ladies across the street are praying the rosary under the grey awning of ancestral plains, burying pasts in graves, a cough here of historic breath, the sounds of children, husbands in a work shed, neighbors on their way to the cafeteria for lunch. The afternoons wallow in themselves, turn to Spring evenings and lights scattered on dark steeples. We are treasures in the sea of white nights drifting near the top of a world, scolded by an hourglass tipped on its side, cottonwoods cast shadows on a bridge wrapped in black silk proud like a man's face. Clouds make eyes in grape patterns hung from a lamppost: they stare at us hoping to know what thoughts mixed with change, hard lives told what to do. A picture postcard from the casino or oak scrub in a sandy field grown up from a place called home by one of the Sisters of Perpetual Adoration. They bloom furious in St. Joseph, Wisconsin while we carry ourselves in chariots with tired horses and three battles a week, enemies like elms in the snow: weighted down, frozen into the immovable spots for barges and island grasses at the foot of golden homes. This land is white like a hundred frosts. We send sunset flashes toward lake shores on the south shore frontier with waves made of hands. Borders broken silver ditches and roots like a ship buried up to its bow with small trees, streets that howl with impenetrable silence.

Sunday April 4, 2004 (Daylight Savings)

Letter from Madeline Island

If I were sick once again, I would think of long lighted days
stuck with you on the island opening can after can of Miller
    High Life
to tell stories of the frozen ponds at the back of your house,
the stumbling uncle from your wedding reception, an old friend
whom you no longer talk to. You played old tunes on a jukebox
and stood around waiting to be asked to dance, rotten odd
moments like complaints or fly by night religions or talk of
    the weather
chill outside, last years frozen spout on top of the water
    treatment tank
with strange stains on its balled feet and rounded silver and
bulging primer coat layered in the thickness from a young boy's
heavy shaken hands. There is an old motel on Bayfield peninsula.
It smells of trout and aged whiskey. The owner is a merciless
woman with holes in her slippers and a cigarette hanging
from a half opened mouth, lipstick on the filter, nicotine stains
on her knuckles. She hobbles to our room with glasses of ice,
seltzer water, a bucket with extra pillow cases, more dry towels.
She once played trombone with the Sweethearts of Rhythm
and married the owner of this land. He built her a motel,
    told her
to run it while he flew around the continent creating new ways
for her to hate him. I scrawl a note on a napkin and tape it to
my leg. It is an outline of a plan to meet you again on the island,
a dream of long distance swimmers struggling toward the sand
and rock of its southern tip where the post office sits with white
painted boards as the small plot of land it rests on erodes further
into the lake. Maybe I will bitterly move away from here. The loss
from back home, the cabin sunsets, the isolation even for birds.
There is a staggered wind, a reminder to crouching farmers.

There is no rest from a wicked life. Even this small land fastened
to the lake could never float away like a piece of driftwood caught
on a heavy wind and northern wave. We are the stationary ones.
We are like islands, free from the mainland, still tethered to the earth.

II.
Europe Like a Forest Praying

Arriving at Atocha Station

When I believed in stars swollen on a dark
train nearer to the sky than we thought,
I prayed on powder blue tiles, magazine racks.
Boys and girls in lines for toys and bread,
edges split with light, glass covered
books soiled in Basque smoke, ash forms
red velvet eyes and sirens. We were all cameras
looking at the sun, silvers and sacred
members with high chins, glory bestowing
nothing on me. What I believed was near true.
A man in a black suit smokes a cigarette
in the gallery drinking a cold beer.
There is a shade of passing light, almost
blurred, the heat rises in our mouths.
We have time for ourselves in bags, small
sections of cloth churning in our hands,
shopkeepers for God, whiskey like the weight
of a rock. I can see the Prado from a clear
window and a roundabout with stairwells,
glass flowers like small crystals held
by an old woman wearing a yellow scarf.
She is worried about her son and buys
a newspaper to pass the time in the heat
of noon after paintings and corners sail
troubled by vendors and yes men. Small
cement statues and corduroy roads made with
cream colored brick as the soft sun loses
its shine in a fountain. We almost weep
like a stranded roar and I was going blind
from the signs in the sky, dark hands
like the orange head of a white swan.
Children go to school in pairs, soldiers dressed
in green and clouds disappearing into
rock ladders, white tiles. I could chase my
painted wall, load a box with this wind.

A Sudden Sense of Panic From Watching a Wasp Wither and Die

Lowly ways withered with scent shaken, without cause.
This wasted breath in light flickered by window branches,
a siren sounded from wings, a finger thin silo of waste.
I witness its slow surprised death on a windowsill
black from a dark chalk outline in a winter silver air,
this raided embrace, a suffocating grope, a deepened
squeeze from a marked immodest tone. The crazy waltz
in a moonlit meadow like a hushed voice in a darkened hallway,
two steps closer to alarm. The ringing of a torso like two fists
suffocating the expression from the face of a determined young
man. The poor creature had struggled against so many hands.

Three Women Who Wept

The first was stranded in a bar.
A large tavern like the round space of a town.
I said, "how 'bout it."
She said, "I wonder why."
The wind would sing whenever
she went to places in her husband's mind.
She told me that America was dead.
I told her America was too alive.
She didn't have enough to pay for a beer.
The bartender threw her out.
Streets belonged to her.
The apartment upstairs did not.

The second mailed me a letter from Spain.
It told of broken arms,
chairs that fell through her legs.
Sermons at a church.
Polite people with deserts for faces.
She saw a man run over by a taxi.
He left stains on the road.
French novels made her weep in front of strangers.
Her boyfriend is fond of children.
She is fond of bruises.

The third preferred fairy tales.
She wished to be a changeling every night it rained.
The family car always leapt onto the driveway.
She wanted the whiskey removed from her house.
It hadn't made her more attractive.
Every year was a little flat.
One day her cat left just like her children.

Elegy for Father Louie

Hearts start ringing padre, with red faces
for God to see. Tell us of trips to Honduras.
White gin in ice jackets, water berries
danced on the tops of tumblers, missions
filled with nuns, two of them never spoke unless
you were around. Then they giggled uncontrollably.
White sacred shawls for marriage blessed
like the rings for wholes of church
goers, friends and well wishers, relatives
who only cry when they are watched.
Put in a good word for Aunt Mary.
She stands at the feet of Jesus and weeps
into an embroidered handkerchief given to her
by her husband, a pilot in the war.
Every time a plane flies overhead she looks
to the heavens and says "hello" to her Albert.
You spoke to her while holding a missal, calmed
her of all her fears, except the ones that
the devil had already asked for. Far light stools
lifted up in other rooms. You almost fainted
at rehearsal, but instead talked to three
other priests who assured you that your
knees would hold up. "She is my favorite" you said.
"I know she is" I replied. "You will do your best,
I know you will. I have faith." You made
the sign of the cross and kissed the small silver medallion
around your neck, the one with St. Christopher
carrying the Christ child across a river. Our journey
will be safe. Shaken hands, glad eyes embraces,
the fathers parade in the back, putting on robes
and combing their hair. We laugh in the sacristy
making fun of Father Tom for being nervous, more
nervous than the bride or even the mother

of the groom. There is a rear view mirror
to the doorway so we can see the congregation,
the dark suits, the doors held open by the wind.
You are surrounded by music and flowers hung
on window wells like boys swimming in red clay
water fallen through to the bottom of the earth.
You were so close to heaven at that time with
your trim eyes and small hands, putting everyone
at ease. I listened to every word you spoke. You told
us stories of foolish youth, smoking behind your
father's broad barn, foul worlds of clowns. Your hands
waved in the air on missions to South America.
It reminded me of the whiskey priest from
The Power and the Glory. Riding bareback through
hilltowns to baptize a child, telling the small children tall
tales of winters in Minnesota. They all stared at you
with wide eyes. Then you were next to me.
Suddenly stepping into the light with a wink,
a nod with a bright haunted look that stuck to raised
archways of the church of St. Peter and Paul.
I remember your hands, slight seas beckoning
the smell of rings and aftershave every day.
You were more than what most men are.
You burned dark into the most sacred of hearts.

To Frank O'Hara in Heaven

This silent morning
statues in my head
of Michelangelo's David.
An east paneled room
brightens facing slain eyes.
Gin and tonics tumbled
over an evening on slant drunken
endtables, bulbs glowing over
a white satin sink.
Social intuition lit her cigarette.
Grey lines carved in
small tiled kitchens covered
in tear stained coasters.
You watch us from
heaven when you
ought to listen
from bed.

For an Old Woman Who Lives in Salema

Her dress read Madam Tayara
around the wind at a white stone villa
on an avenue of olive trees
overlooking the sea.
Her blue wooden face
clapped with frowns
and seaward gaze,
a storm around her eyes.
Handmade metal windchime drawn
clear, shadowed
in the afternoon light.
Sun tribe stars drip onto green water
bruised by distant rays.
She warns the sky to illuminate
like the bright eyes of God, blindly
leading us up the side of a hill
to hide in a well
until the fisherman pull nets
from boat sides, feed the small village.
Brittle waves tilt the shore.
She controls the echoes from the beach
like a gypsy maiden with rings
on wrinkled hands, her hair in knots,
shadows form rock paths,
the smell of eucalyptus.
Her frail back at a recessed doorway,
she turns to disappear into
the Iberian wind.

On Seeing the Ghost of Frank O'Hara at the Louvre

You look so small in front
of the Wedding Feast at Cana,
but who doesn't.
Your white and blue pin stripe jacket
gathers dust, ripe tall ceilings,
well lighted hallways,
marble staircases.

It almost seems that you want to mount
Winged Victory tonight
staring deeply at Michelangelo's Slave.

People watching playing,
looking desperately for the bar.
You see children cling
to each other, a chaperone
on her way to the lui.

A boy stares into the medieval art
glasses, drawn to good looks,
seven ways on Sunday. He is rawboned,
slip and slender on his way outside
for a Camel, the brand
bought at the tobacconist
near Harry's Bar. A chill green cold
line of girls waiting tables,
cider in flutes, lights like
the top of a trio of glasses,
illuminated in the Parisian sun.

You stand at the entrance to an alcove
like you were holding a phone,
your heart always in love.
Keep watching without my help.
I will see you in New York
to talk of art and French food
and parties for performance,
the smoke wisping up to glass ceilings.
You walk away marble footsteps.
What happens is what is done,
left to hang on these walls.

Wed. Feb. 2, 2005

A Garden in Morning: Poem on James Joyce's Birthday

The branches and buildings
still worn
when they fall

And harbour
streets flow unchanged

Your eyes said to see
blackboards
Grace slight breeze

Old lady shiver
on slow black pond

Birds fly with waterwings

Rocks float
churned from the soil
Buckets fill lots

Overcast like an
Irish day, rain spreads
from the west

Plant words
Bury the moon in Zurich

Your garden
a grave for victory

On Being Lead Into St. James Church, Shere

We look under a 12th century font shadowed
by pointed arches, regal like a Baldrick
sash in iron red. Dripping painted pilgrims,
outlines and sights drawn on walls, in grey stairs
frozen like cracks, one for each world
a thousand years. Decorated Norman oak doors,
rounded tombs, slipped borders on gravel
small town roads and a prayer service this afternoon
for the ladies of the lake, simple born BMWs
parked in a moss covered stone gate, headstones
with the names worn from the savage rain
drops on heavy clouds hovering over old England.
We can hear the voice of the Crusaders
of Pope Innocent III, their hands covered in clay,
rippled and cracked edges drift up to the rafters,
wooden crown burns on the legs of sacristy chairs.
The Anchoress's cell seems a view of the altar,
the quatrefoil where she received the body and blood,
said confession. The Brasses filled with rectors
and Tudors, the knights who knelt on early evenings,
the War of the Roses trimming on. Heavy bells ring
on stonework, friction marks, a brooch spire
with nave tales and Horsham slabs, Lychgates
to sway Sirs and Madams home. I bow my head
at the entrance to make amends with the pilgrims.
The air catches the small doors painted with lives,
foretold in plans of travel, desires to atone for their sins.
A spotlight for divine throats with said tales.
The winged angels of light.

Poem Written On A Cigarette Box

Have we gone away
so soon
with smoke leaking
from our lips.

Overturned glass of scotch
slipping into
our bloodstream.

Read as a diary found
in the drawer
of a desk of
an abandoned
house.

This Darkened London

Migrate and sway to temple songs carried
underground,
the smell of music brandished
from the pike of yellow sky.
Folly and ancient flame,
fears from grave dust and the canal in a ring
of green and gold
dragging a slow ripple to the tower.
Black cords in distant blue, cabs
hired to drive past punks
with back alley boots.
Clubs fill up with dark eyeshadow,
now a night of little eyes.
They are quiet, the electric
sputter for flowers and soap, the chemist
for some pills.
Some birds jab brutal.
There runs a dark polish on the street.

Paseo de Orson Welles

The gorge at Ronda was often lit by one thousand hands clapping out white cloth handkerchiefs that moved like spastic doves, bright flickers of feathers, yellow whiskey, ice melted in a hot summer dust filled dusk. The Spanish tile, blue in tides, filmed on Moorish walls nudged a little closer to the edge where the horses were pushed in order to test the depth of each crag so the heavy arched bridge could be dismantled and rebuilt closer to the firepits, the castles, the oldest days of shaped brown rock. Hot sweat summer sun while bulls leapt out of pullied doors into sudden surges of flailed tails and ears. Musty lines drawn in this Andelusian hill town are soon forgotten after watered rusty years, Hemingway's books, famous actors on holiday, full ruffled shirts in the gutter, a matador who stands in the shade of stucco walls and vendors with dark hats urging themselves upon one more afternoon of voices over crowds, thick and full ornate jackets, swords and capes that tell the tales of a small town suddenly thrust into fame by a gorge, a prominent family of trainers, and a tale that tells of a street filled with a river of blood and tradition.

You Will Know It When It Comes, You Will Forget It When It's Over

> *The sun is the best bullfighter,*
> *and without the sun the best bullfighter is not there.*
> *He is like a man without a shadow.*
>
> —Ernest Hemingway
> *Death in the Afternoon*

Last night, you looked youthful, in the moon's bright
    shadowed eye.
Our bed fell on fire yesterday. Leather boots,
Spanish belts in ripped back pockets.
The summer wind hallucinates tethered light,
basement colors for skies grey as cinder blocks,
delicate symbols of clouds puffed into the sky with a
    steam calliope.
You dominate my landscape
You leave me with confidence.

If you are unlucky, you see the brave ones killed,
a punishment for a prideful pagan virtue.
They buckle in the sand like a domineering moose.
A serious, yet noble career in the eyes of a faded season.
The performer (not as guilty as the exploiters)
will learn his trade to rally the public as well as the bookmaker.
We gather in the open air awe and watch serene white edges
of the earth hand-picked by someone with
one good eye, a strong arm, and valor. We pack
it away for long virtuous nights, meditate, entertain,
condition ourselves like bullfighters to
avoid the horns skillfully, to secure a certain kill.
To bow to the royal box with our own scarlet serge.

You look awkward, like a praying mantis.
You look gentle, the coruscation of the centered sun.

Guernica in Flames at the Picasso Museum, Barcelona

Black shed in people's hats,
tired of limping to slaughterhouse prisons.
In war stained glass window eyes cry
tendrils and crown mirrors with surnames,
photos, a white glass covered
sculpture thrice on a floor made with
rock weavers, toothpicks and wooden lichens
cut into floorboards, thick stone benches.
Sweat forms in narrow streets, dirt soaked
gutters, windows. When will the cathedral
scrawl on fire? Everything is darkness when nights
hoist themselves over black and white owls,
incorruptibles in thick molded doors,
the colors spiraling into cubes,
bricks, wander portraits turned upside
down. The faces from the hallways are
covered in shadow, some sun extinguished
into tall ashtrays, shelters of bright homes
provinces of incendiary bombs leak cold blood
from systems, methods, air raids, surrendered
arms and legs from the industry of war.
The Condor Legion flew over Basque
freedom. Bases as far away as Vitoria, Burgos.
Soon the walls blackened with flames.
The wreckage mounds, the shapeless mass
of smoking ruins.

Galway and the Smokeless Pubs of the New Millennium

Long heart like streets and tendrils driven away,
the arts festival moves like a dirty wave. Ups,
and downs to see shops and pubs
after wanderers left themselves underneath
a docket of bricks, dirty bags, small tourists,
grape wine gutterous and dry.
The wishlight of Ireland's west shore,
yellow submarine sculptures, slanted tall grass,
grey silver skies, a tumbled sparrow's ridge on the river
walk next to Nora Barnacle's Bridge.
The streets swell with driven rhythms,
musicians who pause until money is thrown
onto a haunted blanket of new times.
The cows in a nearby field contour in the sun,
with dredged up sunken eyes like
the children who live near Seven Sisters Road.
We are in and out of smog filled patios,
windowed pubs, a demolished old Ireland
without its artisans and journeymen.
Demonstrative, unfamiliar animals dragged,
swollen in narrow streets smoking a fag
clinging us together haphazardly in the hopes
that we will get along, eventually disappear
into the groaning and blurred crowd.
Soon I will pitch myself headlong into the old mist.

Into Europe by Rail—First the Daylight Pulled at Length

1. Madrid

    Atocha is blue and red in Spanish sunlight.
Grey walls plumed by taxis, born over on a likeness
of palm trees, small metal cartoon stools,
men reading walls and searching magazine racks
for the daily shine in train cars. They undermine
    room boards,
terrorists with bombs, bags under one arm.
Ham sandwiches twist themselves with one eye
on the door. Boys running corridors in lime green
light, girls drifted outside hair pins while mothers
clutch to walls like darkness is upon them.
We have forgotten about the days ago,
at sideline ruminations laundered by windows
smoke in small puffs like dragons lying
on their backs, letting cigarettes lilt from sharp teeth.
The heat is wondrous. The chill of metal detectors
makes my mouth ache like biting on tinfoil
or wincing in my aunt's upstairs hallway.
Language is around us in all forms
while children in red jackets huddle together
waiting to be led here or there, a slight
simple lie to get us into a boxcar with windows.
The whiteness blinds us descending the stairs.
Who is here for good? Who will stay in tunnels
for the night to see Picasso in cafés, coffee
grounds on his shoes, a pastry half eaten
in a small ash-can? We set ourselves in brown alleys,
cured hams hung behind, the oil of olives
on trees outside the old city walls, beer with silence,

the vendors too strong to believe in tourists.
The blurred city in outskirts, the heat melting
off the red bricks and white tile lagging in tones,
the shape of the sound of larks.

2. Barcelona

   Nervous light in upstairs landings sunken
   outside. The barges begin to shake when the shine
   hits a small suitcase, a student looking for his chaperone.
   Men in coats, vests, trembling tourists wallowing
   in orange tile and departure screens, little penny
   candy under my hair, yellow wrappers in pockets.
   Youngsters pulling down caps to their white slacks
   at waiting lines too thick to let go of, a faded oilcloth
   on the floor next to a candy shop, a speck
   of tender crimson dropping onto a child's chest.
   We sit in a lounge with light blue walls, mimosas,
   tall high back chairs, the threshold and stir
   of nerves as people pass looking at the ground,
   a cab ride that ended in a small tour. The Columbus
   statue, a blue back seat, a tram to see Dalí,
   Oh! The plans he made in Figueres. The sunlight melts
   into the olive trees while a local boy and girl are wed.
   The parking ramp with circles and wire mesh seats,
   tall sculptures and winding little bells to let the nuns
   know that mass has begun. Knocking on doors,
   a lazy Susan with cookies, graciás sprinkled lightly with
   anise, vanilla rubbed in flour and downed white
   boxes tied with string. The catacombs
   tremble with delight. The searched wooden
   browns and greys limping into small
   grocery shops, Spanish bread, dry cheese
   and milk limped with pictures of soda bread, shrimp,
   vino blanco for nervous mothers on train rides

towards a western home. North by northwest
and planes in cylinder waves. The cathedral is all altars
in semi-circle behind the wave of choirs, limping
old women get coins caught in their shawls.
Far nine makes my mother nervous, the wicker
chairs, the sling back waiters and mugs filled
with leaves from red trees. Someone stands
at the alleyway, the slipped sun is under a cover
of dry light. The selfish students have
given over to museums, corners of old men,
pianos being played under a large Picasso sketch.
Franco sets the sun in whispers and shadows.

3. Paris

Fig fantasies and metro dream wave wonder
in greens and light blue animal glass windows.
The yellow streamers from clear boxes while
tassels shovel over garden parties,
laundry homes and Oscar Wilde's hotel.
The rain seems to fall up and metro stops
sprinkle small mustaches, loud booms,
small children in corners of white tile
playing for small golden coins. Low ceilings,
dark glass drenched in rain, found lines of men,
women in hats, girls worn out in jeans
and boys limping towards machines,
sound light barriers with numbers told
for strangers. There is no color until we are
outside and the sun has frozen itself to
tall statues down the road, the red awnings
overlooking the light dark houses, buildings
that look as if a bomb has sprayed debris
into the cracks of the marble, like spreading
the shards of soft mirrors into glades

of white silken ornaments and left to rot
through centuries. Harry's Bar for a Bloody Mary.
The Louvre is on its heels in the afternoon,
struck like men with umbrellas, the metal
rod stabbed into a glass pyramid heart. I like the
canal, the river that calls Notré Dame from
both ends of its shallow lifts. Everyone is underground
even though we still see them. I can feel the hand
of Joyce at the bookstore, his white wine face
chilled in the cool daylight, a small green corner
dressed in light clear glasses and harboring a cane.
What language and guards trained outside
closets, cigarettes in blue packages with a beauty
of blankets on hills, buildings, slow metropolitan
men worn over light jackets, tree lines, a bustle
like open clear doors and banisters that
twist like rainbows, crepes and German beer.
Take me to Les Invalides and lay me next
to Napoleon, his crimson coffin for our large eyes.
The sound in the afternoon talks like blackbirds,
ravens and the rumple of red wine and cards.

4. London

We seem to be closer in the darkness of dusk.
The pub is what I expected and the people no longer
frighten those ratty children whose eyes are like
supper plates, pudding, dark and deep. Blood from
paper claw alleys, darkness on toe sides of black brick.
Clusters of people on trains, the tube is rounded
out for men in ties, women holding black leather bags,
children who never matter because they are not
as concerned as a parents age. They will not dress
as well, but they had enough money, small
amounts of bread in road stained eyeglasses.

We look up for light where it is only visible
in batches, bumper people with long coats,
rain gear, lighted cigarettes and lunch bags.
The cab stand is full, the ticket man has passed out
under a mound of Herrod's bags, a loaf
of bread sits in the middle of a tram, half eaten,
old and hard like the sun behind its cloud like shield.
The soft slow dirge in a public cellar, a constant
sound of human whispers, small lights blink on,
an echo in wire hung tubes, soot blocks
gleam with rain water. We hear a warning story
of a doctor on the mainland, musicians like minstrels,
logic classes in the rain and hedges blamed
with children sliding on Princess Diana's cement
circle monument. We rush, it seems, in the underground
from Waterloo to Euston to catch a black
boxy taxi to a certain part of the city. Is it headed
toward Picadilly Circus, a reading by Bill Clinton
from his memoirs, a search for shoes, too drunk
to see the spots on the ground or the towers
at Westminster. I talk to the caretaker instead.
Which way will it go? What side of the street has
been painted like a line in this underground,
the grey sky shouldered like the rest of the world,
guarding a sun that never sets on the English empire.

5. Liverpool

The sun in the first weeks of England has landed
in Liverpool, with kind gents in blue T-shirts
hired to direct us north, to the college
and caverns moved next to history. We walk in
echoes, long passages of rail, smokers like
football fans and coffee hounds lounging with
phone booth outhouses, limpid pools of grease

stains dry on stairwells. The cathedral is a rocket ship
pointed towards the sky, the colored light
like a beam from a prism, the wonderful sound
of rain light in puddles on the south platform.
More students, a Hebrew scholar gives us directions
while his pregnant wife slows herself to a bench.
The blue and gold of the city leads to a pub,
the wooden benches worn by Beatles, the singleness
of the city where mist hits our foreheads
with a lilt like a seagull's son. The harbor rents
itself to the land, story like templates
boarded to the shore. The Irish as slaves spent
overboard on their way west, the pond is an
open mouth swallowed by markets of darkness.
A nanny in a white frock, boring into a seaside
town, the walk from routine emotion, candy
floss suppers, axe wielded on the bypass.
Butterfly rain, red and black tiles each with
sparkling faces and metal turnstiles tilted
on the ground. The light is underneath the stairs
and ditches dig rag water, gutters curved
in stations like crescent moons over northern nights.
The ferry blows its horn. The watershed lands
inside the waves and rumbles like the ages.

6. Dublin

Land home state of slider houses, red doors,
a taxi into town while tarts mix at the watering hole
outside Trinity, the bank of Ireland. Boat rides
glare girls in hoop earrings, too much make up
and hickeys while playing the jukebox.
I remember the moon, but today it is the sun
in streamers through large clear and thick doors,
wooden edges rhymed in luster. Shed holes and sighs.

A monastery on a hill and whimpers from children waiting
in line for candy, magazines, red shoes tapped
onto dry white floors, vines from home,
clear plastic wrappers of rain-time.
Left sleep eyed drunks at O'Connell Bridge.
Temple Bar swarms with non-bohemians,
shoe stores, oil spots in rainbows and record stores
for the listening class. Bootlegs and empty
pint glasses on curbs like white shoelaces dragged
from the station downtown windy roads, boxcars
tram guards and car parks. The Celtic Tiger
meows at magazine racks, small bookshops,
cobalt blue buckets from the back of taxis.
He heaves our suitcases into the boot,
tips himself with a hat, a tug at metal rails alongside
quayside streets, the Abbey in middle town,
soon to be moved, burned down from early centuries.
The length of the street is abandoned by homes,
restaurants, Liam O'Connor's publican friends,
home for another wide mouth, a tip of whiskey
and large smiles on wonderful late days.
I think I see Brendan Behan ahead of us.
He is red eyed and blue. Chasing his tale
in the middle of the street. There are people
in alleys, nowhere to duck into. Old merchants with lace,
wine and sweetwood kegs, the minstrels on Grafton
street have never left. We sink into a pub to toast
our vows. To never leave the happy
treachery of travel.